K. Duker & S. McNish
Copyright (c)
1st Print 8/15

ISBN-13: 978-1519150646 (CreateSpace-Assigned)
ISBN-10: 1519150644

Cover Design: Crystell Publications
Book Productions: Crystell Publications
We Help You Self Publish Your Book

Printed in the United States of America

We Dedicate This Book To:

Judy,
Shonta,
Shardae,
Isiah,
Mecca,
Linda,
Terri,
Desiree,
Travis,
and Devin

You Help Shape Our Life.

Acknowledgement

First and foremost we would like to give All Praise and Thanks to God, without Him none of this could be possible. We also want to show our appreciation for the various friends and family members who have been a major support system during this successful financial journey. Thanks to my Business Partner and Co-Author Mr. Shacoy McNish. I have no words to describe how amazing you are! You are a great friend. I would also like to acknowledge Ms. Oprah Winfrey for being a Role Model and positive influence. You are very inspirational! And to all our students that have taken this information and implemented it, changing your lives with it, Thank You! It's you that keep us going. Continue to "Think Rich" and pursue your dreams. Additionally, we wish to acknowledge the countless individuals, organizations, and companies who so generously offered ideas, information, reviewed copies of books and software. "Think Rich" is from experiences, our own and others. Sincerest thanks to all those who have aided an assisted us with getting this book out worldwide. From the pioneers who cut the trails to the engineers who paved the road, so that our travels might be easier. We are thankful for each and every one of you.

Introduction

"Think Rich"

Is the perfect opportunity to give yourself a chance to try something new? It is no need to continue reading this book if you are not ready to reconstruct your old way of thinking.

"Think Rich" is giving you a long term financial perspective on life, instead of forcing yourself to be another average individual (who continuously lives and thinks for the moment). "Think Rich" provides multiple ways on how to produce a steady flow of cash. Relieving yourself from making excuses about how and why you can't accomplish or achieve goals. (Do you want to) learn how to invest your money into things that will make you money? Rather than spending your hard earned money on clothes, shoes and jewelry which are only liabilities.

Stop wasting money now and turn the clothes, shoes and jewelry you purchase into a business expense an write them all off during tax season. (Receive every dime you spent back that year). Here is the chance for you to get on your feet and make opportunities for yourself as well as others.

Spend your time creating new business <u>ideas</u>! Teach your children how to build companies and let their money work for them.

I advise you to react now because if not now it may be too late. Success is waiting for you. Take charge and make the changes needed to be who you have always aspired to become and more.

"Think Rich" is not only a thought process or regular way of thinking, it's also a way of life. All you have to do is keep an open mind. Start reading now and act on what you read in order to have a better tomorrow...

TABLE OF CONTENTS

HOW THE RICH PEOPLE THINK COMPARED TO THE POOR.

CHAPTER EIGHT:

1. **$$$TAXES$$$**
2. How the Rich Avoid Paying Taxes?
3. How to File Taxes Yourself?
4. The 179 Tax Code.

CHAPTER NINE:

1. **OPM** (Other People's Money)

CHAPTER TEN:

1. Step by Step Guide to Build Your Business
   - Hair Salon
   - Barber Shop
   - Car Lots
   - Real Estate Company
   - Online Store
   - Record Label
   - Gym
   - Clothing Line
   - Law Firm
   - Book Publishing
   - Doctor's Offices

CHAPTER ONE
What Is A Corporation?

What is the first thing that comes to mind if some random business man asks you, 'what is a corporation?' The average person will think it's a big building with hundreds of people working inside wearing business suits and ties, correct? Why that is not the case at all. A business doesn't have to be large at all to be a corporation. This is a common misconception among the poor and lower class. Any business can be a corporation, even if it only has one owner. The rich uses corporations to make millions and they normally pay a big law firm a few thousand to do all the paper work for them. Please do not let this discourage you from starting or owning a corporation!

I told you that I'm going to give you many secrets in this book and one of them is how you can set up your own corporation by yourself without paying a law firm any money at all.

A corporation is a piece of paper (that is all)? It is a legal form that the rich uses to organize and conduct business. It has a legal existence distinct from its owner and is considered its own "LEGAL PERSON". Simply put, a corporation can hold titles to property, such as, cars, houses, boats, motorcycles, etc. It can sue people and be sued. It also may have bank accounts set up in its name, hire employees, and do anything else that a human being can do.

Now you see why the rich uses corporations and LLCs (LIMITED LIABILITY COMPANIES) because it is a totally different person than you. Every corporation consists of three kind of people: Those who direct the overall business called "Directors"; those who run the day-to-day business affairs called "Officers" and those who just invest in the business, the "Shareholders".

All of the above groups often boil down to the same person. In other words – a single person can direct and run the corporation, plus own all the corporate stocks, so if you want to incorporate your one person business, you do not have to go out looking for anybody to work for you. But my advice to you is to have other people work for the corporation.

How do I form a corporation?

Forming a corporation is very easy. There are many ways that you can do this. But here are a few simple steps to do it yourself:

1.) Go to any business supply store and ask for an INCORPORATION KIT. This kit will cost you less than 30$. The kit will have all the forms you will need to fill out to incorporate your company, including documents of each state, and your state as well. These forms will take you step by step on how to form your company and also addresses for the **Secretary of the state of each state.** Once you get these forms, you will have to fill them out adding the name of your company, the company type, etc. You don't put your personal information, because, remember, a corporation is a **Different Person** and not you.

2.) You can go online and print all the forms out <u>for free!</u> That would be much faster, if you have a computer at home. <u>Visit www.reference180.com/LLC</u> or pick up the phone right now and call 800-440-8193 ext. 107. Everything that you need and more is right at your fingertips. Plus the website will give you all the inside scoop on how to quickly launch your company and get customers fast.

3.) Google the Secretary of State in your state. For example, if your home state is Pennsylvania or New York, simply google PA or NY Secretary of State and you can call or send them mail and they will send you the forms that you need to start the process. There are no fees for this process. However, you will have to pay the state filing fee or you could always pay a law firm thousands of dollars to do what you can do yourself for free!

I know that this may sound like a lot, but it's really not if you want to enter the **corporate** world and be successful. And no law firm will share this information with you because they want your hard earned money.

This book places the knowledge of incorporation at your fingertips, DO YOU REALLY WANT TO PAY A LAW FIRM THOUSANDS OF DOLLARS TO FILE YOUR INCORPORATE PAPERS WHEN YOU CAN DO IT FOR YOURSELF FOR FREE? This is a matter for you to decide. But I know many people, myself included, that have incorporated without hiring a law firm that may charge you thousands of dollars for this knowledge and work.

THE BENEFIT OF HAVING A CORPORATION

Almost every business and individual can benefit by having a corporation. The risk of doing business nowadays almost makes it a must have. For example, Doctors and dentist could be ruined financially by one malpractice suit, also other professions such as Day-care centers, Bar Tenders, Lawyers, etc. A person that is open for business is open for all types of liabilities, believe me. If you have a business then you know I am speaking the truth.

A lot of people in the hood don't understand this because we don't think outside the average street corner. To make a long story short, a corporation is regarded by law as a separate entity, meaning, it is separate and distinct from you or its shareholders. So therefore, **NO** member or that corporation can be personally responsible for its debts. Sounds great? Right!

Now on the other hand, the corporation can be run in exactly the same way as any other business is run, except that it has many advantages:

1.) If your corporation fails, you may write off up to $50,000 on an individual or joint tax return. Note that this failure cannot harm your personal credit.

Corporations can raise capital by selling stocks in the corporation and stocks can be added, <u>for free,</u> to your company. So, make sure when you set your company up with the Secretary of the State, let them know that you would like a **million dollars' worth of stock added to your corporation.** I assure you that you will be an instant Millionaire on paper. **(THE POOR INVEST IN STOCKS WHILE THE RICH SIMPLY ADD STOCKS TO THEIR COMPANIES FOR_FREE AND SELL THEM TO THE PUBLIC OR TO STOCK BROKERS FOR A SMALL PERCENTAGE).** This is a very important point on why you should <u>incorporate</u> Now! This is how the **RICH** eat and why the poor eat scraps. They have been doing this for a long time. Make sure that if you do not understand something that I am saying, get a stock broker to help you sell your stocks and get <u>immediate cash</u>. Now you see why you need to change your way of thinking. Don't be surprised, but there is a lot more that you need to know. Just continue reading because some of the things that you will learn are going to blow your mind! Oh! You can thank me later. LOL:)

I mentioned to you in the introduction that I was going to give you a few ways to get rich fast and become successful quicker then you'll ever imagine. I also mentioned to you how to become your own Boss and CEO in just a few days. All you have to do is change the way you think and start thinking outside that little pay check you been getting... you working for someone else's corporations right now when you can have your own and have as many people as you like working for you, it's simple! For a minimum investment just paying a State filing fee you can form a corporation today that can save you thousands of dollars in taxes, provide you with a lot of inexpensive benefits, and turn you into an instant "paper" millionaire a position you can take great advantage of to build your actual wealth. I'm going to guide you step by step because I understand all of this information, it may be new to you...

What is a shelf corporation and How Does a Shelf or aged Corporation work? A Shelf Corporation or also known as a (Aged Corporation) is a corporation that was once in business, but a business owner may have lost it for many reasons; A corporation can be sometime best for you because the company already has a Financial History to it or may have been in business for many, many years... a lot of times Banks Love to do business with companies that already have a background other than a brand new Corporation that you just formed... It would be much easier for you to buy a business that was already in existence for loan purposes, credit; you don't have to fill out any forms all you have to do is when you buy a Shelf Corporation is switch the name over to you it's <u>Simple</u>! This Corporation already comes with a E.I.N. (Employee I.D. Number) it's similar to a Social Security number for Identifying your business; every business must have a <u>E.I.N.</u> number attached to their company there is no way you can open up a business bank account without one... a EIN number is a nine-digit number the <u>IRS</u> assigns to businesses for Tax filing and reporting purposes. Pretty much the IRS uses the EIN to identify tax payers... some people use their real Social Security number if they don't have an EIN, but that's not a good choice at all. Personal information & business information should not mix... To receive an EIN number for your business is <u>free</u> apply on line... Directly through the IRS website by going to www.irs.gov/business/Small and clicking "Employer ID Numbers (EIN's) fill out the SS-4 Form and you will get it right away, or you can call at 800-829-4933. But to make things clear the Shelf Corporations already have one so you can save a lot of time filing for one. A Shelf Corporation is very cheap the most you will pay is $150,000.00 dollars the least you may pay is $500.00 the more you pay the better the company you can get; See what kind of business fits you & some company's may still have a high <u>Credit Score</u> so it's well worth the money. To see a list of the shelf Corporations go to the website www.incorp.com I or aged Shelf Corporations.aspx. or call 800-426-2677 right now & chose the company you like whatever's best for you...

<u>The Benefits of Getting a Shelf Corp!</u> Remember a corporation is only a piece of paper; but that piece of paper is very strong in the bank's eyes, for example: if you buy a shelf aged corporation that already has good credit, you can basically get whatever you want under your company name (not your real name), cars, houses, major lines of credit from different lenders, all they want to see is that your company is reliable, and the only way to figure that out is by showing the paper work such as, the Financial Statements, Bank Statements, etc. All of this will be signed over to you once you buy the business.

CHAPTER 2
The Importance Of Having A Bank Account

In this business world, every business man or woman has a bank account to keep hold of their money. Having your money in the bank is one of the safest places you can store your funds. One of the reasons you should have a bank account is to grow interest over the years. Essentially, you are establishing a report with the bank. Plus you can receive many rewards from purchasing items with your bank card. One of the greatest mistakes I made when I was younger was never opening a bank account, instead I held all my cash in a shoe box under my bed like the average street guy does, for example if someone was to break in your house and take all your money you worked hard for its really nothing you can do to get your money back, "you just have to take that one as a loss." But on the other hand, having your money safe in a legal bank, it's secured no matter what; even if you become a victim of identity theft, your money is insured by the bank you can always get it back (trust me).

How to use the bank in your favor! Using the banks in your favor is pretty much having the banks work for you. Once you open up an account with the bank they automatically work for you. The banks are big corporations, a big money business that you should want to be a part of. A lot of people don't know how the banking system works because you never took the time out to open up a bank account in order to see & learn how the banks treat their customers; without you banking with them it's no way they can ever make any money. Make sure after reading this chapter you go immediately open up a bank account and get yourself a good banker at your bank that you can always talk to, become a friend, and ask him or her questions about all the loans they can get you. Bankers have major access on getting you all the money you need; they can get you all the best loans, mortgages, repos on cars, and much more. Having a banker as a good friend or in your phone call log it will be so much easier to get the loans you need. A banker is one of the best friends to have in the business game. Just be honest with them, they can help you out big time, even if your credit is bad.

Quick Story: one day I walked into a legal bank and asked to speak to the bank supervisor. She asked me if there was a problem sir: I replied "No ma'am, I just needed her to appoint me a good banker that can be my mentor and keep me updated with all the great offers you guys have to offer me. The young lady said no problem and sent one of her bankers to help me out. From that day on we became great friends; anytime I need a loan she did all my paperwork for me & got me all the best loans that I could afford, loans that I didn't even know existed. Believe me it works, try it, and you can thank me later.

The difference between a business account and a personal account: With a business account, you can't open up one unless you have a business or a corporation like I mentioned earlier in chapter one. A business account is for all your business funds to be held, and a personal account is for all your money that you're really not using that much, except for paying all your personal bills. A business account can be used to pay all your bills for your businesses & also pay off debt that you may owe. Paying bills directly from your business account will create a Trade line which is a paper trail so that it could be much easier to keep track of your payments, the good thing is; everything that you buy from out of your business account or checking account is a tax deductible at the end of the year, meaning if you was to buy a computer for your business that cost $1,000.00 you can deduct that $1,000.00 on your taxes using the 179 Tax Code and get every dime back on your Tax Return. So honestly you never lost any money at all... (Sound great right)? Keep all your receipts in a safe place even if you go to a restaurant to eat out, it's a free meal for you because you're going to get that money you spent back come tax time. That's why the rich stay rich, everything they buy is a tax write off ... and the poor stay poor because they're biggest mistake is not having a bank account, they buy everything with cash thinking that they ballin' hard... keep all your receipt's and turn it into cash come tax time... believe me it works... so always remember keep your business account separate from your personal account, one thing you don't want to do is mix all your money into one account.

How to use your checking account: At your bank you should have a Business Account, a Checking Account and a Savings Account. Business Account to place all the money for your business only, a Checking Account to write off checks to pay others business only, a Savings Account to stack up all your profit and investment or in case you may need money for an emergency... Make sure your bank gives you a check book for your company and, a check book for your personal use. Quick note: Make sure before you write a check to any company or store you have enough money in your Checking Account, if not your check will bounce, meaning it could be rejected a few days later and you could get in deep trouble for writing a bad check... **Please avoid making THAT mistake.**

What is Over Draft protection: Just in case you didn't know you could get an Over Draft Protection: on all your accounts... ask your bankers about the overdraft protection, this will protect you from over drafting money from your bank account. Normally determined on what your credit score is, will determine how much overdraft protection you can get. So for example: If I open up a Bank account at my bank and I have 1,000 in my bank account; I tell the Banker that I want the overdraft protection on this account, now whatever your credit score may be this will determine how much you will get approved for... so for instants my credit isn't that good at all, I may only get approved for $200.00 or $300.00 dollars overdraft to my account; so instead of me having $1,000.00 now I will have $1,200.00 or $1,300.00 to spend; you will have to pay a little percentage but it beats being charged a BIG FEE for taking over the original amount you had in your account; Basically, to make it sound more simple; If you had overdraft protection on your Bank account with $1,000.00 in your account and you get approved for $1,000.00 now you have $2,000.00 instead of a thousand. It's simple now you have more room to play if need be. I advise you to get the overdraft protection on all your bank accounts now its extra money for you; you never know when you'll need it. So set it up now if you don't have it these are all the great benefits the banks have to offer that they won't tell you about unless you ask so React Now!!!

So now what's next? In the next chapter, I want to teach you how to avoid the middle man and get whatever you need directly from the source.

CHAPTER 3
"How to Avoid the Middle Man"

Having knowledge of a particular matter means everything. Basically people charge you for their knowledge. Most people just want to avoid doing things themselves or may just don't know how to do the work that's needed. In life everything cost a price rather you know it or not; but the key of this chapter is to save as much money as you can; because if you don't know certain things it will be much easier for someone to get over on you and over charge you a lump sum of money ... So pay attention carefully while I take you step by step on how to avoid paying extra cash.

"Secrets that the car lot owners won't tell you"

The first thing the car lot owner does is ask you what your Credit Score looks like, right? This determines on how much you will have to put down on a car or truck. If your Credit is good; then you can drive off the lot most likely not having to put no money down. And on the other hand if your credit is bad you will have to put down a big down payment; that's just the way it is... The banks are the original owners of the cars but the car lot owner gets them for a cheaper price for having a dealership license, pretty much the banks front them all their cars for a way cheaper price then what you will pay the car lots must get the banks approval before they sale you a car. Whenever you buy a car off the lot with a car note you have to pay a payment every month this is a contract between you & (the consumer) and the seller (the car lot). If you was to stop paying your car note or miss some payments your car will get put on the repossession list; so if the repo man gets a hold of your car it automatically goes back to the bank and the repossession will go on your Credit Report and damage your Credit Score. It may be hard for you to get another car unless you pay the entire cost which is not good. So to make a long story short, always cut through the chase and go directly to the bank & ask them to give you a list of all the cars that's in repossession; you can buy them or lease them from the bank instead of going to a car lot who originally work for the banks, not all car lots work for the banks but majority of the major car lots do; Such as: Lexis, BMW, Dodge, Mercedes Benz, Ford, Cadillac, etc... So for example: before you decide to buy or lease a new car from a car lot, first go to your bank and ask them could you have a list of all the vehicles that's in repossession. You may see something you like and get it for a way cheaper price... a 2010 Range Rover SUV will cost you $54,000.00 off the lot and if you agree to pay a note every month, by the time you pay the car off in a few years you would have paid way more than $54,000.00 because of the interest. Now if you go directly to the Bank you can buy that same Range Rover for way less than $54,000.00 & save a lot more money. A lot of people don't know that the banks own cars, houses, boats, motorcycles, etc... Cut out the middle man and get you an expensive car, boat or house for cheap!

<u>"How Business owners get loans off your signature"</u> Your signature is very powerful so be careful on some of the things you sign such as <u>contracts</u> or any legal documents; I just explained above that once you agree to pay a certain amount of money a month for a car, house rent, mortgage, etc... this is a legal contract between you & the seller or renter agreeing that you're going to pay a particular amount each month; once you sign that contract your locked in for how many years the contract stipulates &you can face a few penalties if you void the contract agreement. Your word is everything & your signature means a lot; The car dealership, for example, has thousands of people under contracts to pay a certain amount of money to their business each month. That's a big amount of money corning in for them, you do the math... All the dealerships have to do is take a list of all the people they have under a contract agreement and take that to the bank and get a huge <u>loan</u> just off your name & signature. It's called (Account Receivable). The Bank will easily give them the <u>loan</u> because their Financial Statements tells it all; How much money they're receiving each month from you & thousands of other people. All the banks want to see in order to get a loan is how are you going to pay them their money back. So

once they see that you can get a loan for pretty much whatever amount of money you need. The dealership pays off their loans with our money that you pay them each month so that they never come out they're pocket at all. They use you to pay off the banks... The money you give them each month ... The dealership may be paying $150.00 a month for the car you're driving now; but you paying them $320.00 a month, so they profit $170.00 off you and only give them back $150.00 that's business.

In this chapter I want to teach you how to avoid paying extra money. The same method applies to mortgages, if you're not the first mortgage holder. If you don't buy your house through the bank someone making a profit off of you! For example: I bought a house from the bank, a 4 bed room home, for $100,000.00 I put only 10% down which is a thousand, now I only owe the bank $90,000.00. I'm paying 5% of the mortgage each month to the bank which is only $500.00 I can choose to pay it myself and live in the house with my family; or instead I can rent it out to another family for more than the $500.00 I'm paying. I will rent the house for $900.00 a month, pay the bank its $500.00 and I pocket the $400.00... you see how I played the middle man? You also can do the same thing. In chapter (5) I am going to show you how to get good AAA credit in 60 day's so you won't need any money of your own; you can get whatever you need on Credit without using your own money, it's called (OPM) Other People Money. In chapter (4) I am going to teach you about all the loans you can get and how to get them easy.

CHAPTER 4
Getting Loans Easy:

Getting loans easy is not hard at all; there are many kinds of loans you're entitled to get as long as you are reliable and trustworthy. Having a good perfect credit score will get you just about any loan you need; in this chapter I will give you a huge list of money lenders that you reach out to & get loans in case you may need one. Personal Loans, including debt Consolidation Loans, Small Business Loans, Venture Capital to start up your company or Expansion of your business, mortgage and Real Estate loans, grants, and much more. To make things simpler, you could look in the newspapers, yellow pages, Wall Street Journal, for money Lenders. You can google Money lenders & you will have access to hundreds of money lenders in your town, that's willing to loan you money, so start looking now...

What is a Business Loan?

A business loan is a loan you will get for your business not for your personal use. If you have any great business ideas write out a business plan with all of your ideas, how much money you'll think you need for your business, make sure your business plan is done professionally not hand written; but typed up and take your business plan to the bank. If you present a nice plan the bank will invest in your idea. Also once you form a corporation like I explained to you in chapter one you can also apply for a business loan to start up your business. You can get up to a <u>several hundred thousand dollars</u> for business startup money, that's just another option just in case...

What is a Personal Loan?

A personal loan is for your personal use it can be for whatever you choose to do with the money such as: pay backed up bills, pay off Credit Cards, take a vacation, buy a car, etc... you can take out a <u>personal loan</u>; many people make Signature Loans for whatever much you may need; some banks even offer Unsecured Loans by mail. All applications are treated with confidentiality. If you are interested in this type of loan contact your bank right now! <u>For example:</u> another way to get a personal loan is a <u>Secured Loan</u> meaning, you can put up something for Collateral, such as: House Deed, Car Title, or even your own money that you have in your Savings Account could be your collateral: If you have $500.00 in your Savings Account you can ask your banker for a loan for $500.00 and you can use the money in your Savings account as Collateral; they will give you $5.00 dollars cash in your hand put a freeze on your $5 dollars in your Savings Account. As you pay the loan off the money in your account starts to become unfroze. So if you pay $100.00 dollars towards your loan $100.00 in your account will come available to you, this is one of the best loan methods there is & it will build your credit sky high! I will get more in-depth in this method in chapter (5).

What is a Home Equity Loan? Home equity Loan can be a great way of getting money; a person's home may be their biggest investment. For example, if you buy a house for $100,000.00 you now have $100,000 equity in your home; the more you pay on your home the more equity you have, if you paid $45,000.00 into your home after a few years of paying your mortgage each month, you will have $45,000 worth of equity that you can get a loan for, it's really all your money you put into buying your home, this is called Home Equity Loan or you can get a Home Equity line of credit as well; if this is something that you would like to do then call your banker NOW! You can take the equity out of your home and buy another house with the money, rent it out to a family and with the rent money they pay you with you can pay off your home Equity Loan. Sounds Great right? It's easy! Simple...

What's next? In this next chapter I am going to take you step by step about the importance of having credit.

CHAPTER 5
Credit

What is your meaning of wealth? Is it a stack of $50 and $100 bills in your pocket or under your bed? This is the concept a lot of people have when they assume a person being wealthy... Honestly to be real with you, real wealth is not a stack of 100 dollars bills or you walking around with your pockets full of money or even having a big stash spot in your house, that's a poor man mentality or better yet a street Hood' way of living. The typical millionaire don't carry around any cash with him at all; so now the big question becomes how do the rich buy anything they want and walk into all the finest stores, restaurants, banks, Country Clubs, or airports in get the best service in the world? Why do people always run to the rich man aid at the slightest nod of his head? The answer to this question can be answered with one simple word; <u>Credit</u>. The rich can get cash whenever they want at any time, but they choose not to work with a lot of cash laying around. The rich man's signature carries the same value as gold, this is why they never carry cash. I told you in the very beginning of this book that I was going to give you all the great secrets on how to get rich fast, but first you have to start thinking smarter than before, if you really want to be wealthy. If this is not what you want then I advise you to <u>shut this book now</u> & continue doing what you been doing thinking poor, but I advise you to continue reading because I promise you to enjoy the same type of credit reputation if you pay close attention and follow me step by step in this chapter. A lot of people think that the only way to get great credit is by paying all your bills, being on time with all your payments. Most people build their credit up slowly over the years by paying all the bills on time, that's good, I know differently. You can enjoy all the benefits of a millionaire's credit reputation in 60 days or less no matter what's your present situation. In this chapter and the next chapter (6) I will give you various plans you may use to build your credit up high and get rid of all your old <u>bad debt</u>. But this time you will use credit to get yourself wealthy.

What is credit?

Credit could be anything but the true definition of credit if you was to look it up in a dictionary it will tell you that credit is "reliance on testimony; Faith or to sell or lend something to someone. Money possessed to you from a lender, and a trust to repay back the funds. Everyone knows the best credit anyone can have is credit at the bank. Now you can use the bank credit to purchase assets that's going to make you plenty of money in return. The rich use credit to buy money producing assets such as houses, invest in business etc. Majority of the people when the banks send them out preapproved credit cards for $5,000.00, $10,000.00, $20,000.00 or maybe $50,000.00 and spend it up as if it was free money and buy all kinds of liabilities like shoes, cloths, go shopping for the kids buy a car etc. None of the above things will produce any type of income to repay the <u>Bank</u> back its money, so now you max your credit card out now you wondering how you going to pay your credit card bill each month. A lot of people make this big mistake. Use their credit cards in get in great debt and take many years to pay it all off. The rich is different in this matter, they take advantage of major credit cards use the bank money to buy assets, the assets will make them money to pay off the loans, so really it becomes FREE money to them, money that was fronted to them and took great advantage of it. The banks will continue to increase your credit limit when you pay more than the minimum amount each month. So many people are lost when it come to the true meaning of credit, and if they do know the true meaning, they don't take advantage of its benefits. Use your credit to purchase incoming producing assets, okay, the rich love credit.

<u>Good Credit:</u> Having good credit will get you just about anything in this world especially when your credit is AAA-1, no one will ever deny you anything. Creditors find you to offer you money, major credit cards, thousands of dollars preapproved car loans etc. The credit game is a big business it's just like selling a product. So the banks and lenders find people to give them credit so that they can make some

money off you, it's no way the banks will make any money unless they give out credit and loan 1 they make their money off the interest. So they need you to make a profit. The rich take advantage of their good credit score and use it to get anything they want in this world, that's why it's so important to take care of your credit and keep your credit score high.

Having good credit will get you all the best credit card deals, interest rates, Annual Percentage Rates (APR) etc.

Having bad credit could be very difficult for you to even get a cell phone in your name, having no credit could be good credit and also it could be bad credit as well. Having no credit at all is a good start off because you can build it up to something tremendous, having no credit at all is a great start off for you because you never "burnt your bridges" with any banks, and on the other hand it could be a bad thing not having any credit because you will have to start off most likely with small credit cards lines with only $250.00 or so. I will teach you How to get great credit if you don't have any credit now. Start applying for credit they have to offer you no matter what the limit may be. Take that money and make a purchase and pay off the full amount of whatever you brought that same month, this will build your credit limit further when you pay over the minimum amount due. Always try to pay more than you have to pay, go above and beyond this is how the rich get down. While the poor only pay the minimum amount and drag the entire process out to pay back. Do this method with all your credit cards you have with the department stores, it works, believe me all you have to do is be responsible and make sure all your payments get paid on time.

Bad Credit

Bad credit is a terrible thing to have, it's nothing you can do having bad credit, because you choose not to pay your bills on time or you just refuse to pay period. Most poor people with a poor mentality get credit from family, friends, banks, lenders etc... and refuse to pay it back, a person with bad credit really tells a lender that you're not trust worthy, at all. Everything works off credit now-a-days, so if your credit isn't correct then it's nothing you really can do unless you be one of them slicksters that try to get everything you want in other people's name to ruin their credit. Millions of people in America suffer from Bad credit, deep in dept. Its many ways to get out of bad debt and fix up your credit such as, Debt programs that will help you manage your funds to pay off all your debt. It may take many years for you to fix your credit. In the next chapter I will give you a few secrets on how to fix up your debt faster than ever. From here on out I advise you to start being more responsible, it is no need for me to give you these secrets if you're going to continue to be careless. I worked hard for many, many years studying business, financing, credit, and much more because I wanted to become a business consultant to help others such as yourself. Knowledge cost, and many business lawyers will charge you thousands of dollars for just the information I'm giving you in this chapter. With Credit Repair Companies, but the majority of them just want your money & will tell you that they are going to fix your credit up and never do. It's not about the money with me, it's all about me wanting to help others become successful. It's no way that you can become successful with bad credit so here's a few tips how to get an AAA-1 credit score fast. Number one rule: pay all your bills on time. Never, never go past your due date. Rule number two: get things in your name such as phone bills, car, home, cable etc. One of my favorite secrets to establishing a great credit score in the matter of weeks, here is how you do it: I mentioned to you before that the best credit anyone can have is the credit at the bank. Now you can use the bank's money to not only have credit at one bank, but you can have as many Bank accounts as you wish. My advice to you, I want you to start out with $1,000.00 dollars to execute this plan. If you don't have a thousand dollars then you can do it with $500.00 at the least. Take your $1,000.00 to your regular bank, or a local bank that's near you, it's your choice. Open up a savings account, wait about 3 day's to make sure your account has been posted. Next Step: Apply for a loan for whatever the amount of money you put in your Savings Account $500.00 or $1,000.00, offer the bank to put your money in your Savings account for collateral. So if you have a thousand in your account, I want you to get a loan for that thousand dollars. When the banker hears you're willing to use your money in your account as collateral they will give you the loan with no questions asked. Why is this? Because this loan would be risk free for their bank. Now you have $1,000.00 in your bank gaining interest and $1,000.00 in your hand. The bank will place a freeze on the $1,000.00 in your savings account, but this is no worry at all to you as of now.

Next step: I want you to take that $1,000.00 to a second bank and open up another savings account with the entire $1,000.00. Three days later, see the loan officer to arrange for a $1,000.00 loan, again I want you to use your Savings account as collateral just as you did with the first bank. I want you to go through this procedure with at least 5 different banks. You can always do the same at other banks in your area even though it may not be necessary.

Next Step: After you have opened a Savings Account at 5 banks, and obtained loans at each bank, I want you to take the $1,000.00 from the last bank and open up a   Checking Account at any one of the banks you choose, a few days later I want you to begin writing repayment checks. Pay one full month's payment at each bank at which you have taken a loan, one week later make another payment to all the banks. At this rate, you will have your loans paid off in about 45 days or so. Understand with each payment you make, an equal amount of money will be "unfrozen" in all your savings account. You can take this money and place it all into your Checking Account as you go along I promise you you'll be surprised how fast your credit rating goes up no matter what your previous rating has been before. Now you are wondering why you have more than one bank giving you a credit reference, how great is that? Better yet, which may sound even greater after making a few payments, the banks will automatically clear you for future signature loans at their banks, and will give you a wonderful credit rating at all the credit bureaus who checks your credit rating. I told you I'm going to teach you how to be your own boss but for the time being you can hold on to your job while working this plan. Quick Note: (1) always take your Savings account book with you whenever you're applying for loans. This is something the bank offices will want you to have; and (2) always try to get at least a 9 month repayment schedule for each loan, this will give you enough room to pay back, even though you will pay each loan back much sooner. Don't worry about the interest on the loan because the interest from your Savings account earnings will pretty much cover that. Basically you're paying a very small fee (price) to get a great credit rating. After you have worked this plan, and get a great credit score for paying off all your loans before time, the banks will see that you are trustworthy. It's all about establishing a good report that's all. Once the banks see that you are a person who pays off Loans with many different banks, you can apply for credit cards and bank cards and have no worries of being denied; Remember, you are backed up by the most important credit references of all banks! You shouldn't have any problems ever getting major credit cards such as: American Express or Chase should pose no problem. This plan could be done in as little as 45 days if you do exactly what I told you step for step, believe me I've done it. One thing to always remember: you have a great credit rating now, so from here on out keep your credit rating high by paying all your bills 8, loans before time. Start now.

"A few secret's the credit agencies won't tell you"

There are 3 major credit agencies that the majority of businesses deal with 1.)Equifax 2.)Transunion 3.)Experian; it's also another credit union that's involved now that may have your credit report called (Innovis)... a lot of people pay these companies to receive a copy of their Credit Report each time they apply for one. By law under the <u>FCRA</u> (Fair Credit Report Act) you are entitled to receive a free copy of your credit report every 12 months at no additional fee. The credit agencies won't tell you this information unless you ask, other than that they can charge you to get a copy of your report at each credit union Experian, Transunion, Equifax and Innovis. My advice to you is to get a copy of your report every 3 months at each credit union within the year so this way you can be up dated with all your bills, and keeping up with all your payments, making sure your creditors are posting your payments on time.

Another secret the creditors won't tell you: <u>For example!</u> Say you have a credit card at Macy's each month on the 30th day Macy's will send a report to the top 3 agencies letting them know your payment history, rather you made your payment on time, if you didn't make your payment at all, or either you made a payment that was late. Pretty much to sum this up it's like a credit report that the creditors give to the credit agencies about you, the debtor. Even if your payment was late it will affect your credit score but they won't tell you this information!! So make sure each month all your bills is paid on time or 3 days before, this will build your credit score high. My advice to you is to always keep it honest with all your creditors you'll be surprised with some of the things they will do for you such as lower your monthly payments if you don't have the money to pay, give you a few months to pay if you're going through a financial problem. The worse thing I see people do is try to duck the bill collector when they call or sent you a piece of mail, it's their job to do this, and it's your job to pay them their money, but if you don't have it by law no creditor can force you to pay something you don't have at the moment, all you have to do is be honest with them, they will actually help you out, but they won't tell you this information unless you bring it to their attention! So answer your phone or write them back in the mail and explain to them your problem. Communication is everything! So make sure you open your mouth if you need help. If not all the creditors are going to do is report that you're not making any payments to them, so this will give you a bad report each month and this is how people's credit goes bad because they duck paying their bills instead of talking things out with their creditor. Please don't be ashamed to ask for help if you're in need. Communication is key!

The difference between business and personal credit:

As I already explained Business Accounts and Personal in the previous chapter Accounts; to make a long story short. Business Credit is your company credit that one would have to build up just like it was your personal self. The only difference between the two business credit the highest score is about 90 and the lowest is 0 (zero). Personal credit goes as high as 900 determined on what credit agency you use. You can have a FICO score 750-800 and have a score from Aquifax 700, Transunion score 650 and Experian score 850 but each agency may view you differently than the other your FICO score should be the greatest out of them all, any credit score under a 600 is poor, 650 to 700 average - good, 700 to 750 and up is excellent credit. Get your credit score today and see what your credit rating is. Even if you never had anything in your name still apply for your score. Some creditors look at a person with no credit as being good credit. Use the method I gave you dealing with all the banks to build your credit score high. Set up your corporation as I showed you in Chapter One and start building your business credit score. Remember your business is a different person then you, it can apply for loans, pay taxes, get sued and sue other company's business name, not your personal name or personal credit cards. Quick note: "use a separate credit card for all your items. Credit interest for business purchases are 100% deductible while interest for personal purchases is not. Using a separate card for business purchase will help you keep track of how much interest you've paid for business purchases. Honestly, their card doesn't have to be in your business name, it can be one of your personal credit cards also, but I rather you use a business company credit card but if you just starting out you may want to use your personal credit card to buy all your business supplies. Please make sure you keep your receipts so you can use them for a business Tax Write-off! Go to www.Annualcreditreport.com to review all your credit reports from each agency at once for free! WHAT'S NEXT: In the next chapter I'm going to teach you about debt and a few simple secrets on how you can increase you debt.

CHAPTER (6)
Debt:

There are two kinds of debt; you have debt that is good and debt that is bad. As far as the debt that is good it is the money you borrow from any lender and use that money to buy growing assets, these assets should produce income for you to pay off your lender such as, Homes that you buy and rent out for a bigger profit then you have to pay each month. This type of debt is considered as a good debt. As far as bad debt basically its money that you refused to pay back to your lender rather it be a bank, money lender, personal loans, a family member or even department store credit such as, Macys, Wal-Mart, Best buy, Home Depot, etc. Having a bad debt will destroy your credit report and score. So if you are willing to enter into the credit world you having a bunch of bad debt will get you nothing, I'm just being honest with you. Millions of people all over the United States is suffering from bad debt and pulling their hair out not knowing how to get themselves out of the big jam. In this chapter I will give you a few tips that will help you get out

41

of your <u>debt</u> sooner than you think. The inside scoop that your creditor won't tell you is that once you stop paying them their money they put a bad report out on you to destroy your credibility from getting anything else. It's a <u>bad look</u> on your behalf, you can agree too that!! I bet you will? After you have missed 3 payments or more, the creditors look for collection agency's to sale your debt for pennies on a dollar. Pay close attention while I take you step by step on how this process works.

<u>Step one!</u> If your creditor gives your debt to a collection agency. The creditor hires professional people such as these collection agencies to try to collect the money you owe to the creditors, these people work on their behalf 90% of the time. Collection agencies buy your debt for a way cheaper price then what you originally owe hoping that they can get out to pay them something. Some collection agencies will even go to the max to get you to start paying something they may tell you just give us half of what you owe, or even say just give us $20.00 a month. Collection agencies are willing to take anything you have to offer.

<u>Step two:</u> your original creditor will stop calling your phone and sending you letters in the mail after they sale your debt to one of the collection agencies. The creditors sale your debt because they rather get something then just taking a big loss form you not paying them anything, so they sale it (your debt) for pennies on a dollar. Now you have to deal with these agencies.

Step three: by law once these collection agencies receive your debt from the <u>FCRA</u> (Fair credit Report Act) to see a copy of the <u>contract</u> that you originally had with the creditor. The collection agencies don't have your contract because you never entered into any agreement with them, so most credit repair and debt repair business all they do is dispute the claim that you don't owe money and if the collection agency says that you do owe money, then tell them "then may I have a copy of my client's original contract?" By law all creditors have up to 30 days to provide the proof after your dispute to get rid of your debt, if they cannot prove that you are the one who owes them money, then they have to take it off your credit report. Disputing things on your credit report will immediately go into investigation; it may take up to 45 days for you to dispute the process. They will then notify you of the results. If you are a victim of Identity Theft please let all your creditors know that someone has stolen your identity & to put an alert on all your credit cards. Take a look at your credit report every 3 months from each of the credit agencies and review your credit report; if you see anything that does not belong to you by law they will have to remove it after their investigation. So my best advice to you is avoid going to credit repair company's you can do the work yourself from your home this will save you thousands of dollars. Remember if your debt is in collection tell them you want to see your contract it's no way that they can prove business was done between the two of you, because honestly you never did any business with the collection agency, you did business with the creditor.

What is Debt Consolidation?

Debt Consolidation is an easier way to control all your debt at one time. Debt consolidation programs will actually help you pay off your debt by dealing with the creditors personally on your behalf. Debt Consolidation Programs will take at least 2 years to get you out of all your debt but it's worth trying if you're suffering in a big debt jam. Debt Consolidation programs will help get all your payments lower so that it could be affordable for you to pay your payments. I will show you how this process works. For example: If you were to get involved in a debt consolidation program it will cost you a fee each month determined on how much debt you are in. Some people even pay thousands of dollars each month to debt consolidation programs to get them out of debt within a year or two. Anyone who signs up for this type of program it may show up on your credit report. This could be a bad look for you, if you was to try to get a credit card from a creditor. Creditors pull your credit report before they give you a line of credit and if they were to see that you're involved in a debt program it will raise a red flag instantly! It shows that you don't know how to handle your money properly, so majority of the time they won't deal with you unless their desperate. Some creditors may give you a chance but give you a very, very high interest rate on the line of credit they give you because you're a big risk to them. So let me show you step for step how to consolidate all your debt by yourself without going through a debt consolidations program.

Step one: Take one credit card that has a very low interest rate so that your payment each month will be very cheap on that card.

Step two: Get in contact with all the creditors that you are in debt with and negotiate with them for a better monthly payment that you can afford to pay them. They will love to do that for you since you haven't been paying nothing, do this with all your creditors.

Step three: Transfer all your payments to that "one credit card" that has the low interest rate, so all your debt will be consolidated to one monthly payment instead of having many monthly payments with different creditors. This method is called Debt Consolidation. Quick note: All your creditors will take a minimum monthly payment off your credit card each month that you agreed you can afford. Now you're starting to pay your debt off for way cheaper then what you originally was paying!! Each month all you have to do is pay the minimum amount each month on that one credit card, so within two years or so your credit will be not just good but great again. As time goes by you will see a big difference with your credit score changing as you make your monthly payment on time each month. I told you in the beginning of this book that I promise to help you out no matter what. All you have to do is listen closely and start reacting now! You can thank me later!

What next? In this next chapter I will give you a few marketing secrets to build up your company fast.

CHAPTER (7)
Marketing:

Marketing is a strategy tool that every business has to use in order to get your business or product known to the public. Marketing is one of the greatest tools to make your company successful. In this chapter I will give you a few tips on how you can make your business or product successful quick. Many business owners go out of business within a 5 year period. Reason why because they didn't have the correct marketing strategies to make their business become successful. Once you open a business just know that you are a competitor to other businesses who share the same kind of service. The key concept is what could you do to make your business or product better than other competitors? Marketing is a strategy that you have to go to the drawing board and write out. Marketing is a plan and one thing you don't want to do is make one of the biggest mistakes people make in business; that is not coming up with a marketing plan for your business. Most people open up businesses without a plan on how they are going to get the masses of people to hear about their company or service.

Once you incorporate your company, place an ad in the Newspaper in the business section with the name of your business, what your business does, your business phone number, and a quick 20 to 30 word saying to draw people to call your business for example; Hidiyyah's Hair Salon address: 1021 Board St. Phila PA, 19106, Phone: 215-222-2222, website: www.Hidiyyah Hair Salon.com, "Best Beauty Salon in Town" call today and get a free hair wash and blow dry   and 50% off of any hair style you like, all stylist is "top of the line"

Placing your business in the papers will be looked at by thousands of people each morning. Everyday people view the business sections in the papers so make sure you market your business in the papers.

Second step: Radio, marketing is another great way to get your company noticed by the public. Marketing your service on the radio station is easy, a radio blast your company for only $200.00 or so a week. Radio marketing strategy has thousands of listeners that listen to the radio each day that will hear about your business. Quick note: every dollar you spend on promoting your business is a tax write-off! So make sure you use the company credit card or company checks to pay for your promotion and if you choose to use your personal credit please keep hold of all your receipts and write a note for your receipt for what the transaction was for. In chapter (8) I will teach you more about taxes and how you can receive the majority of your money back you spent for business purposes.

Third step: Business card & Fliers: Business cards will help blow your business up and it will make you look more professional, always keep boxes of business cards to hand out to people you come across. Have a nice business card that describes your business and profession and a picture of your business logo. Most promoters use fliers to promote their businesses.

Quick note: Always leave business cards & fliers in other businesses to help promote your business. Some business owners will allow you to do this for free! One of the things I used to do when I was trying to get my company off the ground, I would pay a few young kids $20.00 to hand out my fliers in people's stores and mail boxes throughout the City. A lot of neighborhoods supported my company because when they called they were surprised at some of the deals I was giving to the customers. In marketing it is also treating your customers well, because if you provide them great service and be polite, your customers will always spread the word about your business. Rule #1: Treat the customers well, the customers are always right. It's not all about the money being first, the customers will bring you all your money, as long as you treat them well.

Fourth step: Posters: Posters of your company also can be a great marketing strategy. Place posters on city light poles on buses, trains, intersections, and if you can afford it (which I will make sure you can after reading this book), I advise you to place your poster on billboards on the main highway in your town thousands of cars drive by billboards and read them. I had many people who called my company and said that they read about my business on a billboard while driving to work.

Step five: Word of mouth: Spread your business around to people-people have conversations about your business with family and friends and co-workers at your day time job when you're just starting up. People love to run their mouth all day, every day, so mentioning your business will get around town faster than you think, "people talk," remember that. Please don't be afraid to open your mouth when it comes to promoting your business. Tell a friend to tell a friend and give them a discount on every person they refer to your business. People love discounts, so make sure you do referrals, this is a quick way to draw people towards your company.

Step six: Social media: Online advertising has become one of the biggest marketing tools for most business men and women. Advertiser's love interactive marketing because it is more effective and more targeted, while also being less expensive than traditional media. Many big companies use online marketing. Kimberly-Clark launched Huggies pure and Natural diapers without TV advertising to reach a more targeted audience for moms. Quick Note: An important question you evaluate where you're going to spend your marketing dollars what are the most effective ways to advertise online and what kind of results should I expect? Online advertising skyrocketed in 2000, reaching $8.2

billion then dropped with the dotcom bust and leveled out at $7.3 billion in 2003. Since then the market has been great and it's expected to grow even larger within the next few years. In 2010 it reached approximately $12 billion and expected to grow up to 17 billion in 2014.

Emailing: Email continues to be very strong and effective; it is a means of communicating with customers by offering them discounts, introduce new products, and services, facilitation improved customer service and much more. Email marketing is growing because it has many benefits:

- Email marketing can integrate other types of media such as video, audio, and social media.
- Programs could be implemented quickly to provide immediate results and sales.
- Email marketing is an effective way for people to pass information along to others.

Email marketing is a great tool. I advise you to use to promote your company, it is widely used and accepted by both businesses and consumers. The cost is nothing to use Email marketing. Let me tell you the top three benefits for social media ranked in priority are

1.) Increasing exposure for your business
2.) Increasing traffic/subscribers.
3.) Building new business partnerships.

People spend 20 hours or more per week on the internet. So start promoting your business or product now online!

Facebook: Facebook was launched in 2004 as a Social network exclusively for Harvard students. Within four months, 30 colleges had joined the network. As of today there are more than 300 million active users from 170 countries. I use Facebook to promote my businesses. Reports tell us that Facebook is the number-one Social networking site. Over 4 million users become fans of Facebook's public page every day. The average user has at least 100 friends linked to their site and adding more friends each day. My advice for businesses that want to tap into the power of Facebook, it's very important to apply a few marketing basics. First of all, understand that the audience on Facebook is still young men and women, especially more heavily towards females. So if you sell power tools, Facebook probably won't be your first choice in building your brand or company. But if you are thinking like Victoria's Secret, you will have great success. Hair salons, barber shops, clothing lines, book publishing, car lots, houses, real estate, and entertainment are all good for marketing on Facebook. Most people use Facebook to play around and chat with women and men vice-versa, that's cool but when it comes to your business you must stay focused to that and network with people regarding your business. Come up with a strategy and stick to it, always have a marketing objective. Like any other marketing strategy, social media strategy is developed to affect the actions of the target audience you wish to reach. All you have to do is be consistent and I promise you, you will get your business known to the public.

LinkedIn: Facebook and Myspace are extremely popular and have a larger audience of people, LinkedIn is a very good way business professional's use to network and market their business. It's also an effective network for communities, associations, and organizations. This website is a key benefit that not too many people know about. LinkedIn has grown to over 52 million members. This will be a great networking service for you. For example: You will have to set up a profile page which generally includes information about your company and service or brand, basically whatever you have that you are promoting, and you should place your company or brand and work experience. Many people use LinkedIn for finding new jobs and careers, to seek referrals and endorsements, and to give referrals to others. When people want to hire an individual with specific kinds of skills, they might ask for recommendations from people they trust in their network. This is the site you will need to promote your hair salon, barbershop, publishing company, real estate company, clothing line etc... The more you use it the more people you will connect with from all over the world. All you need to do is invest your time to add connections. Most people don't go outside their neighborhood to do business that's why their business never grows. Start connecting with people outside your town and you will be surprised when you see how many people will come support your business if you give them a good reason to. Give and ask for referrals, and keep your profile current and basic, nothing to <u>extreme</u> ... You can also start or join a group to connect with people in organizations, associations, and universities to build your network. My advice to you is to please just participate in the groups you join. If you're about getting your company out in the public then speak up so that you can be heard, if you don't say anything then no one is going to even notice you or your business. You can comment or start a blog post, make announcements to the group, ask questions to help with research, and participate in many other ways. All of these things will help improve your business (Believe me)... If you just started your business and need help to build your company or brand, then LinkedIn is for you so make sure you get involved now. Don't wait until later.

<u>Twitter:</u> If you believe in a fast, quick shortcut way to get things done, then you will love Twitter, a microblogging service founded in 2007. Twitter is growing faster than any other networking service. Within a year, more than 2.2 million accounts were generated. People use Twitter to ask questions; "What are you doing?" With far ranging topics from eating a piece of candy to announcing a new product or service. They also share information about people, companies, new stores, products, really just about anything. Many big business men and women have Twitter followers such as; Oprah, Obama, all celebrities love Twitter. It is also used for raising money for charities and promoting your company or brand. Twitter is a great marketing channel I advise you to use to build your company. It is very easy to build your business and network with different people.

Many small businesses are quick to use Twitter now they have an army of followers. <u>Quick Note!</u> The way you build is through personal customer communication, community interest, social causes, and being a helpful resource to people. I use Twitter to build my army of followers. Use the retweet function, which is a lot like forwarding an email to people in a database. Twitter also has other business resources you can use to build your business or brand. Guy Kawasaki is the author of several bestselling books and CEO of Garage.com. He works with early stage startups. He offers more helpful hints on how to use and optimize Twitter. He has a huge following, he is also qualified to be a great Tutor for Twitter. Go to the source!

GuyKawasaki.com, all the advice you will need. Such as; How to get thousands and thousands of followers, how to reach the masses of people you'll never know who can help you and how, making a defocusing market strategy both plausible and profitable, ways to increase the followers you already have, Tweetdeck to create and follow a search, Twilert.com for email notification of search results, How to spread the word about your company. The worst thing a person can say is "NO". 177 people signed up, and another 280 signed up for a free copy of Kawasaki's new book, Reality Check, totaling 450 people. These people had 140,000 followers. Can you deny all this free marketing? Log on now and you'll see what I'm talking about. You can thank me later for giving you all this great information for free. I'm not going to charge you nothing, all I want in return is to hear that you became successful.

People use blogs because they get value from the content, not because they are being sold something. A Blog gives likeminded people an opportunity to talk directly with people who share similar interests, and post many ideas about specific topics. Both marketer and business owners gain much value insight from his or her blog posts, which he or she updates almost every day. I use to ask myself what people really get out of blogs and writing blogs daily. At a minimum, you will have the opportunity to connect with people and an opportunity to talk to people directly. One thing I'm going to need you to understand in this business corporate world it's all about networking and connecting with different people. Those who you know, and those who you don't know. "It's not what you know it's who you know!" I have met many people who I haven't even known for a month that connected me to people who they knew who shared the same kind of project I was working on, we exchanged ideas and we became great friends soon after and worked on building our projects together. Some of them became my partner, some of them we just exchanged ideas on how to get rich. But for the most part, blogging is a great tool to use if you really want to meet the right people for your business... Seth Godin is a best-selling author when it comes down to marketing books, including permission marketing, "The Purple Cow", and many other marketing books. His books will have your businesses all over the world in weeks, I advise you to get his books to be more knowledgeable on this topic. Both marketers and business owners gain insight from his blog posts, which he updates almost every day. People learn from his blogs, he connects with people and exchanges ideas. If you are interested in learning more, you can click on links to buy books or even have him personally to give you great advice. Godin is also the founder of Squidoo. Squidoo is a very great opportunity to exchange your ideas and topics. It's another way to build your company and passion. Quick Note: The point of Squidoo is not to sell something, but to engage.

Digg: Digg is another type of social media service mainly for book marketing that can be used to promote new stories about your company. By sending an article to customers and potential customers, or posting it on another website, people can choose to Digg (or promote) a story if they like it. Digg can be used to build your company brand. Digg has over 30 million users a month, so you can communicate with customers, prospects, or anyone who may have suggestions or ideas for your company. If you are a Digg member with a profile, all your information is launched on the first page, creating instant fame for you and your company. Like Twitter, Facebook, Myspace, and Instagram, Digg is also a channel to build up your brand or company.

Stumble Upon: Stumble Upon is another social book marketing site, which helps users find and share websites. When clicking the Stumble button! The network delivers pages matched to your personal preference. These pages have been recommended by other search engines because they are rated by members and sorted by personal interest and preferences. It has over 8 million users. Another nice benefit of social book marketing is that tags help search engine rankings. To learn about other social book marketing sites, consult the social media tools section in the Social Media Strategy and Planning Guide (www.marketSmarter.com).

Blogs: Blogs are booming in popularity as a public relations and marketing tool. Technorati, a blog index, cites that more than 133 million blogs have been written and posted by people and companies to reflect on different topics, events, or news stories. Over 900,000 people write and post articles every day. Businesses don't create blogs to necessarily sell products or solutions, even though this is often the outcome. Quick Note: The main purpose of a blog is to connect users and readers with their personal brand of a person or company. Entertain and find people who share your passion and interest. When your blog is well written and executed, this becomes a very effective marketing strategy for you. Here are a few tips to improve your blog strategies. Before you create a blog, always define your blog strategies ad process. You will always have to update your blog one to five times a week. Pick a blog topic to talk about, submit you're URL and RSS feed to blog directories, and search engines. Share your knowledge and expertise with others in your industry. As you're networking increases, you will see other bloggers who reference your material or link to your site. Promote and market your blog as you would a product or service. I advise you to include the blog address or all of your business cards and other marketing materials. Market your site using social media networks and through channels that can post your blog within a larger portal that is relevant to your target audience. You should also research high-ranking blogs and websites and exchange links.

Other Advertising Resources: Infomercials free production only pay on sales. Basically this site will promote your product and service for free and get paid only if you make money, sounds good right? (Smile) You can call now at: (800)509-9961 or visit www.marketforcetv.com. Another great one is www.send2press.com, they do press release writing and get targeted newswire distribution since 1983 with CEO. Another company will help you get at least 10,000 visitors to your website, delivered to your web! Only $1.99 to www.thebestadvertisingsite.com. Now that I have given you all the major ways to market your business, you should not have any excuses why your company shouldn't be the best in town if you utilize all of what you have read in this chapter. Advertising is the most important and that's why I dug very deep to get you all the connections you will need to build a successful business. Please take great advantage of these opportunities and start getting to work now! I really believe you can,- make it in this corporate world, with all the knowledge I have given you in this book, It's no possible way you can lose out unless you are one of those people who just want to work a 9 to 5 daytime job for somebody else's company, breaking your back for others. I understand that everybody isn't meant to be a Boss or a CEO even with me giving you the game on how to be a boss and CEO step by step. Some people just don't want it, and I say that because I've seen it many of times where people had the opportunities right in their face to be their own boss and turned it down and said, "I'd rather work for someone and get a paycheck" rather than being the boss. They say to me being a boss and running a company takes too much time and energy. I say to those kind of people, only if you know what I know you would hasten to be the boss rather than being the worker. Always remember this! If you have to put in a lot of work and time in your company every day, then you're not a boss, you are actually a worker. A boss dictates his company from a distance while he hire's Directors and Supervisors to run his business for him. This is something that I understand very well. I was a worker for many years but now I'm happy to say "That I'm a Boss" and I don't do any work at all. All I do is sit back in my office with my feet up and come up with new ways of how I can invest my money on bigger and better projects. I work smarter not harder, and if I can do it, then I say to you brother or sister you can do it too, because I'm no better than you. All this poverty for what? You have all the information you need right before your hands, so use it. Nothing will excite me more but to hear that you took all this great information and put it to action. Start off by incorporating your company today just the way I explained in chapter one.

What Next? In the next chapter I will give you some secrets on how the rich avoid paying taxes, how to file taxes yourself and many more tips you can use regarding taxes.

Chapter (8)
Taxes:

If you are a professional, no one needs to tell you that taxes are one of your largest expenses. The more you make the more the IRS takes from you during Tax time. Overall every human being who has a business or a day time job must pay taxes on the money that's being made. The best way to minimize your taxes and maximize your take home income is to take great advantage of every tax deduction available to you. The IRS will never complain if you don't take all the deductions you're entitled to, and it certainly doesn't make any sense of advertising ways to lower your taxes. In fact many professionals miss out on all kinds of deductions every year simply because they aren't aware of them, or because they just neglect to keep records necessary to back them up. In this chapter I'm going to touch on a few thing's you'll need to know about taxes, and keep things as simple as possible so that it could be easier for you to comprehend and understand okay? This book is the first of its kind, so now I'm going to show you some things you may have not known. My goal is to make April 15 as painless as possible. <u>Quick Note:</u> Even if you choose to work with an accountant or another tax professional, you still need to learn about tax deductions. No tax professional will ever know as much about your business as you do, and you can't expect a hired professional to search high and low for every deduction you might be able to take. Especially during the busy tax preparation season. This book could be your legal companion, but it's always good to have an accountant on your legal team to make things faster and easier for you. I don't want to confuse you at all, sometimes taxes could be very complicated, but I will assure you that you are not going to pay more than you need to with the IRS.

<u>A few secrets on how the rich avoid paying taxes:</u>

<u>Step 1:</u> <u>Forming a nonprofit organization:</u> A nonprofit company is not conducted or maintained for the purpose of making a profit. A nonprofit company can be a service that serves the purpose for helping people, and all the money that's being used is to support the organization "only". For an example of a nonprofit organization is a Masjid, Church, Halfway House, or just about any kind of service you want or like. Oprah has a nonprofit organization to support the poor kids in Africa. It does not have to be a big building or a big company at all. Simply it's the same thing as a corporation only a piece of paper. You can be the owner of a nonprofit organization to control all the transactions within it, but it does not affect your personal credit if anything was to go wrong. This is how the rich use their

nonprofit organization company to save on taxes. <u>For an example:</u> When you have a company, a LLC, or Corporation, say your company made 100,000 this year, 25,000 was for all your business expenses, bills, equipment, rent etc... So you have 75,000 net profit. Instead of getting taxed on the entire 75,000 which is a big lump sum of money, the rich will pay himself a salary 30,000 from the 75,000 before being taxed which leaves the net profit of 45,000 left over. He will take 20,000 from the 45,000 and <u>donate</u> it to his nonprofit organization which leaves only 25,000 left to be taxed instead of the full 100,000. Money that's paid to yourself has nothing to do with your business taxes. You will only have to pay taxes on a regular 1040 from just as any other worker will.

You will get that money back during income tax time when you file taxes for yourself. The 20,000 to the nonprofit organization which still belongs to you is non-taxable funds. All donations are not taxed at all, and to make it even better, that 20,000 you donated is a tax write off for your company and you will get that back as well when you file your company's because this money can't be taxed and is a business write off for them so they get the money they donated back and still have access to the money that was donated to the nonprofit company belonging to them. So instead of being taxed on the full $100,000 you will only be paying taxes on $25,000. The rich avoid as much as they could, and so could you if you follow what you just read step by step, you will save a lot more money instead of giving it all to "Uncle Sam".

Step 2: Setting up a Health Savings Account (HSA): Health Savings Account is another tax advantage method of buying health insurance and has been available since 2004; Health Savings Accounts (HSA's).

Quick Note: Although (HSA's) can save you a lot of taxes, they are not for everybody. WHAT ARE HEALTH SAVINGS ACCOUNTS? The health savings account concept is very simple. Instead of relying on health insurance to pay small routine medical expenses, you pay them yourself. Basically to help you do this, you establish a Health Savings Account with a Health Insurance Company, bank, or any other financial institution. All contributions to the account are tax deductible. This means that every dollar that you put into that account is a tax write off for you, and you don't have to pay tax on the interest or other money you earn on the money in your account. You can withdraw the money in your HSA to pay almost any kind of health related expense, and you don't have to pay any tax on these withdrawals. In case you or your family get really sick, you must also obtain a health insurance policy with a high deductible. In 2008, at least $1,100 for individuals, and $2,200 for families. The money in your HSA can be used to pay this large deduction and any co-payments you're required to make. Using a HSA can save you money in two ways:

- You'll get a tax deduction for the money you deposit in your account.

- The premium for your high deductible health insurance policy should be lower than those for traditional comprehensive coverage policies.

To make things simpler for you, you may individually establish a HSA for yourself and your family and pay for health insurance out your own pocket, or when you set up your corporation or LLC (Limited Liability Company). You can have it establish a HSA for you and make contributions to your HSA on your behalf with business funds and this is also a tax write off from your business to you. In either event, there are a few rules that must be applied to participate in the HSA program, you're going to need two things, a high deductible health plan that qualifies under the HSA rules, and HSA account. That's pretty much it. Quick Note: If you are young and enjoy good health while you have your HSA and don't have to make many withdrawals, you may end up with a substantial amount of money in your account that you can withdraw without any penalty for any purpose once you turn 65. Any other retirement accounts, HSA provide a tax break when funds are deposited and when they are withdrawn. No other account provides both a "front end" and "back end" tax break. With the IRS you must pay tax either when you deposit or when you withdraw your money. This account can be an extremely lucrative tax shelter. For more information on HSA please go to the IRS website at www.irs.gov or by calling (1-800) TAX-FORM. Or consider getting "The NOLO 4th Edition Tax Deductions for Professionals by: Attorney Stephen Fishman," author of the best seller on taxes. His book will help you understand many tax deductions that I can't explain in detail in this concise book.

WHAT IS THE 179 TAX CODE? If you learn only one number in the tax code, it should be Section 179. This humble piece of the tax code is one of the greatest tax boons ever for small business owners, including professionals. Section 179 doesn't increase the total amount you can deduct, but it allows you to get your entire depreciation deduction in one year, rather than taking it a little at a time over the term of an asset's useful life. Which can be up to 39 years. This is called first year expensing or Section 179 Expensing. (Expensing is an accounting term that means currently deducting a long-term asset. Example: In 2009, Abdul buys a $4,000 photocopy machine for his business. Under the regular depreciation rule, Abdul must deduct only $400 the first year, $800 the next year after and $800 throughout the next 5 years. The photocopy machine has a life line of 5 years. This is called "Depreciation Deduction", but deducting the copier under Section 179 instead, Abdul can deduct the entire $4,000 expense from his income taxes in 2009. So he gets a $4,000 deduction under Section 179 instead of the $400 deduction he gets using depreciation. My advice to you is to take the 179 tax code now, because of inflation and the time value of money. It is often better to use Section 179 if you can, to get the largest possible deduction for the current year. The most you can deduct using the 179 tax code is 25,000, many business men too great advantage of this tax deduction so the tax code has a limit of only 25,000. This method can only be used once a year. This is for all of your businesses combined, not each business you own and run. As long as you meet the requirements, you can deduct the cost of Section <u>179</u> property up to the limit discussed above, no matter when you buy the property or service during the year.

<u>Quick Note:</u> You cannot use the 179 tax code if you use the item less than 51% of the: time for business use, if it's an intangible asset such as patent, copyright, trademark" or business good will, if you brought it from a relative, or if you inherited the property or received it as a gift. For any item that falls within one or more of these categories, you will have to use regular depreciation instead of Section 179. Section 179 lets you take your total deduction up front in one year, while depreciation requires you to deduct the cost of an asset a little at a time over several years. The slower depreciation method isn't always a bad thing. In some circumstances, you may be better off using depreciation instead of Section 179. But if you want every dime you spent on an item the following year, then Section 179 is for you. To make a long story short, if you were to buy a $3,000 computer for your business, you can deduct the full $3,000 under the Section 179 tax code and still have your computer after you get your money back during tax time. It's like you got the computer "for free". For more information about this tax code 179 please go to the website www.irs.gov, you can thank me later!

<u>HOW TO FILE TAXES YOURSELF:</u> During tax season millions of people are running around town trying to

figure out who they can get to file their taxes for them in order to get a nice amount back on their tax returns. Many people hire other professionals or tax services to do all the work for them: Well in this chapter, I'm going to show you how you can avoid paying tax services hundreds of dollars when you can do the work yourself. You don't have to be a professional tax expert to handle this job. After reading this section, you can even start your own business during the busy tax season. You can start off by filing taxes for your family and friends and charge them a small fee for doing the job. Here's How You Should Do it:

Step One: Gather up all your expenses for that year, all receipts, bills, all your recent payments to other businesses, receipts you spent for food, gas, clothing etc... Separate all business expenses from personal expenses.

Step Two: Gather up all your income from all your jobs or businesses for that year. To manage this more easily, go to your nearest stationary supply store and buy an expense chart and an income chart. It's a booklet you can keep in your car or home. It has a list of all the columns. All you have to do is mark it off each time you spend on something, date, place, and total amount, and what you spent the money for. You also have a chart called the "Income Chart" where you would mark down all your income you received. Each day you can do this and at the end of each month you can add up all your expenses and all your income.

Recording your Expenses: Recording your expenses is what we normally think of as "Keeping the books". Every business should have a record of what it spends and what it earns. Without this information, it will be impossible for you to know how much profit your practice earns (if any); and it will be much more difficult to prepare your taxes. Most professionals use accounts or bookkeepers to perform these recording functions. However my advice to you, if your business is small, you could do it yourself and save the money. Resource: For an excellent overall guide on how to do small business bookkeeping yourself, refer to "Small Time Operator" by Bernard B. Kamoroff (Bell Springs Press), a fun and good read for you. There are also many simple financial programs such as those like Quicken and MS Money that work off of a computerized checkbook. Greater account software including MYOB Account Edge and Plus by MYOB, Peach tree Accounting by Peachtree Software, and Quickenbooks and Quickbooks Pro by Intuit. The software can accomplish more complex bookkeeping tasks, such as double-entry bookkeeping, tracking inventory, payroll, billing, handling accounts receivable, and maintaining fixed asset records. Quick Note: If you're only using a program especially for your type of practice, such a program will probably cost more, but it won't require much customizing for your particular needs. There are many specialized programs for accounting available for every profession. If this may sound too difficult for you please consult with a bookkeeper or accountant about these programs. After you have gathered up all your expenses and income, the IRS requires that you have documents to support the deductions you list in your books and claim on your tax return. If you don't have any proof for what you are claiming on your tax return, an <u>IRS</u> auditor may conclude that an item you claim as a business expense is really a personal expense, or you never brought the item at all. Either way, your deduction will be disallowable. You may hire an accountant to work for you to record all your deductions in your books, but you <u>must</u> document your deductions yourself. You need to learn the <u>IRS</u> documentation rules and live them each day. The most common business deductions- travel, meals, and entertainment are all tax <u>write offs</u>, but you must show proof for all your transactions.

<u>For Example</u>: If you go on a business trip you must show documents to support that business trip, name of company or person and reason why you took the trip. Every dollar you spend on that trip is a tax write off. Same-thing goes for when you go out for lunch to talk business, you may write that meal off on your taxes. So keep all your receipts. Every deduction should be supported by documentation showing what, how much, and who. This is what your supporting documents should show:
- What you purchased for your business.
- How much you paid for it
- Who (or what company) you bought it from

<u>Quick Note:</u> Keep hold of all canceled checks, sales receipts, account statements, credit card sales slips, invoices, or petty cash slips for small cash payments. All of

the above will be a big help for your tax write offs. If you choose to do your own taxes with the IRS or any of your friends and family, before you send in their documents, make sure everything is supported by proof. If you do all the adding and subtracting yourself, or by using a program on the computer before sending your documents in to the IRS, put all your deductions on one piece of paper. This will make it easier for the IRS to calculate how much money you will receive on your tax return! Always remember, keep your business and your personal expenses separate.

<u>HERE ARE A FEW GREAT SOURCES YOU CAN USE:</u>

IRS Telephone Information: The IRS offers a series of pre-recorded tapes of information on various tax topics on a toll-free telephone service called TELETAX (800-829-4477). See IRS Publication 910 for a list of topics. You can talk to an IRS representative on the phone by calling 800-829-1040.

IRS Website: The IRS has one of the most useful internet websites that many people neglect, because you may have not known about it. Among other things, almost every IRS form and informational publication can be downloaded from the site. The internet address is www.irs.gov. The IRS has a special section for small businesses and self-employed, (www.irs.gov/businesses/small/index.html).

The IRS publishes over 350 free booklets explaining the tax code, called IRS Publications ("Pubs" for short). Some of these pubs are very easy to understand and some are very difficult to understand. You can download all the booklets from the IRS website at www.irs.gov. You can also obtain free copies by calling 800-TAX- FORM (800-829-3676).

FREE IRS PROGRAMS: The IRS offers small seminars on various topics, such as, payroll tax reporting. You can ask questions at these half-day meetings, which are often held at schools or Federal Buildings. You can call the IRS at 800-829-1040 to see if programs are offered near you and to get the IRS Small Business mailing list.

OTHER ONLINE TAX RESOURCES: Instead of the IRS website which may be something new to you, there are hundreds of other privately created websites on the internet that provide tax information and great advice you can use. Some of this information is very good; some of it is just ok. A comprehensive collection of web links about all aspects of taxation can be found at www.taxsite.com. Other useful tax web link pages can be found at:
- www.abanet.org
- www.willyancey.com/tax-internet.html
- www.natptax.com/tax-link.html
- www.el.com/elinks/taxes

Some useful tax-related websites include: www.accountantworld.com, com/tax/filing., www.taxguru.net.

NOLO'S WEBSITE: Nolo maintains a website that is useful for small businesses and the self-employed. This site contains helpful articles, information about new legislation, book excerpts, and the Nolo catalog. This website will be a very great service for you if you're looking for specific information for business people, as well as legal research center you can use to find State and Federal Statutes. The internet address is www.nolo.com. There are many books you can buy on taxes that could help you comprehend more better especially for the average person. The best books known dealing with taxes, individual taxes and small businesses. Two of the best are:

- J.K. Lasser's Your Income Tax(John Wiley and Son's)
- The Ernst and Young Tax Guide(John Wiley and Son's)

You can find a list of these publishers at www.wiley.com/wileyCDA/ Section/:d-103210.html. If you need any help, or find what you have read in this chapter difficult to understand, please consult with a tax professional, you don't have to do your own tax research. There are hundreds of thousands of tax professionals (tax pros) in the United States ready and eager to help you for a price. A tax pro can answer your questions, provide guidance to help you make key tax decisions, prepare your tax returns, and help you deal with the IRS if you get into tax trouble. If you have any questions for me I would be more than happy to answer your questions. Become my friend on Facebook at: Shacoy McNish, and I will give you all the assistance you need. I will be your friend, I will take the time out to listen to you, and make you feel comfortable. If not me, I will direct you to some tax pros who already have clients in businesses similar to yours. A tax pro already familiar with the tax problems posed by your type of business can often give you the best advice for the least money. Your relationship with your tax pro will be one of your most important business relationships. At www.naea.org, you will find all the best people you'll need on your business team.

WHAT'S NEXT? In the next chapter, I'm going to show you ways how you can use (opm) "other people's money" to build your empire.

CHAPTER 9:
Other People's Money (OPM):

One of the best secrets of becoming wealthy is using "other people's money" (opm). It seems that all of us have the drive and ambition to obtain wealth. So why would so many of us literally work ourselves to death for large corporations while trying to make a living? To be fully honest, it is that very few of us will ever get wealthy working for someone else. To get wealthy, you simply must have your own business. However, most people lack the foundation of a new enterprise: "Capital." With the necessary capital, almost anyone of average intelligence can become wealthy. If you don't have all the funds you'll need to start up your business, in this chapter I will cite to you many methods of getting you all the capital you need by borrowing "other people's money" (opm). The secret of becoming wealthy in any enterprise is to use (opm). Opm is simply other people's money. Yes you need other people's money to build a fortune. Many people are lost when it comes down to using (opm) to get what you want. The most logical way to obtain opm is to borrow it. Borrowing money has been the "key" to all really great fortunes built in this country and around the world. The rich people have been borrowing money to become wealthy, no one became rich overnight unless opm was used either by way of banks, lenders, financial companies, etc... The wise men use their lenders and buy income producing assets. They do not use the money to buy liabilities and personal items. Borrowing opm must be done correctly. For any reason if you use and handle money poorly or unadvisedly, my advice to you is to find another course to take. When you use a lender of money wisely however, funds borrowed can be the gateway to a better lifestyle made possible by investments and their resulting earnings. Use borrowed money properly, you would not have any problems paying a loan off if you use the money in the proper way. Borrowing can help give you a better home, a new car, fabulous vacations, and many other great luxuries. But always remember! These advantages must come from the earnings made by your borrowed opm, not from the loan money itself, and the earnings must also provide interest payments on your loans.

STEP ONE: Use Personal Loans: If you don't have a good credit score, already, then I want you to use the method described in the previous chapter to develop a good credit score. You will most definitely need to borrow capital to finance your venture. The easiest type of loan to get is a personal loan. After establishing a credit reputation using the method described in chapter five, securing a personal loan should be no great problem. Business loans are usually harder to get than personal loans, especially from a bank. If you have no business experience, business loans are doubly hard to get. So a personal loan should be your first choice when applying at your bank. The bank will feel more secure to give you a loan then your business, because if your business falls short then you cannot be held accountable for the funds personally unless you sign a clause stating you will be held reliable for the funds if your business was to fall short. Most banks, when giving business loans may have you sign such a clause for security purposes. Quick Note: An easy way to get around this is to go to the bank and apply for a personal loan. Do not tell the loan office that you are borrowing the money to finance a business. Otherwise you will be subject to a different set of requirements, ones that are much stricter.

Let the bank know that the money is for a major car repair, home investment, or something else that would require an appreciable sum such as you are requesting, (This could not be said to be illegal, since after you could change your mind after obtaining the loan). If you need a loan right away and have not had time to work the credit plan outlined previously, you may need to employ a co-signer.

This may be a friend or relative. Another way you could do this is to pay a co-signer. Many times businesses with immaculate credit reputations will co-sign a note for a fee. All you have to do is convince the co-signer that you are a good credit risk, but this is not a difficult thing to do. Remember you have an account with five different banks; if you chose to get a personal loan- this is a very easy plan to work once you have established yourself in the credit world using the plan in chapter five; Here is how you get the money: 1). Go to all the banks you have opened up an account at and get a personal loan application for each. 2). Fill out the application in the banks, all in the same day. 3). Fill out each application, requesting a $5,000 personal loan. 4). If you have established yourself, you wouldn't have a problem getting the loan at each bank: If all five banks approve you for the $5,000, then you will have $25,000. Take that money and make your investment.

BUSINESS LOANS: We have already mentioned in the previous chapter about business loans. Getting a business loan to start up a business is not all that easy but it could be done. I have already explained that getting bank loans with which to begin an enterprise to borrow money to improve or extend an existing business, you should already have in mind how the money will provide increased profits, to better pay back your loan. Be able to explain- on paper and verbally what you will do with-the money and what the results will be. Know just how much you need and exactly how it will be used. This is all the information the bank wants to know, so I'm just giving you the heads up now so that you can go in ready and prepared. Quick Note: Be able to demonstrate how it is to be employed to generate increased income. Also make sure you provide proof of how the loan will be repaid by showing your income file, financial statements, or pay stubs if you are working at the moment. Don't worry! On any loan application you pick up, you will find yourself becoming more acquainted with a business loan requirement collateral is always "key". So, although your business may be limited in worth, your personal net worth may need to be used to support a repayment agreement. Remember, even if your business is not in the best of financial shape, if you can show a game plan that is reasonable and believable, you are going to have a great chance of getting your loan approved!

GOVERNMENT LOANS: If you are trying to build a foundation in your business, and you feel that some kind of government loan might be the right route for you, look to the "Small Business Administration" (SBA) program for help. This program could help you start your business. This program has a "No Risk" factor. Look for the phone number of the (SBA) under the Federal Office listing of your telephone directory. Before I end this chapter, I just want to assure you that you will find all the money you need by using (opm). There are so many money sources out there just waiting to give you money for your project, all you have to do is look around. Read the papers, look online for money lenders, there is a lender out there waiting on you to call, believe me! One way to get a quick private loan is to pledge your personal property. There are many non-profit organizations that will make loans of money if you pledge personal property such as gold watches, antiques, etc... They normally give up to $3,000 or more. You can search online for their organizations. The funds you need are out there, all you have to do is look! Now that you have read this book I hope that you enjoyed everything useful to help you build a successful business. What you have read in each chapter was concise and straight to the point so it could be understood by the average person who doesn't know anything about business or has not experienced having their own company. In the next chapter I will end with a step by step guide on what you need to do to start up your own company. Each business you start should be formatted the same way.

CHAPTER 10
Step By Step Guide To Starting Your Own Company:

STEP ONE: Establish your corporation by getting all the forms from the Secretary of state(your state) or this could be done online as I explained to you in chapter one. Before you form your corporation or LLC (Limited Liability Company) you will have to come up with a corporate name. A name that has not been taken by another corporation. A good name that identifies your practice.

STEP TWO: You have to get an Employer Identification Number (EIN) from the Internal Revenue Service (IRS). Simply call the Holtsville NY, service center, and they can issue you one right on the phone or you can get one online at www.irs.gov/business/small and clicking "Employer Id Numbers (EINs). Fill out the SS-4 form and you will get it right away. You can call 800-829-4933 and get one over the phone.

STEP THREE: When you receive your corporate packet in the mail you will have to utilize the tax packet you have. You'll need to register with the taxing authority. The packet has everything you need. Make sure you get a sales tax certificate. Even if you don't sell anything, you can use it as a sales exemption certificate for things you purchase in connection with your business.

STEP FOUR: In most states you must have a Board of Directors. This could be one or more people. This person directs the overall business. I advise you to choose yourself and your mother or someone you can trust to be a director of your company.

STEP FIVE: You need to appoint officers who report to this board. This can be a President and CEO and a Vice President, an officer that is there who can run the day-to-day business affairs. This person can be you and you also can choose another person to be Vice President. I advise you to hire someone who you think will be best to represent your company.

STEP SIX: ESTABLISH A CORPORATE BANK ACCOUNT: Doing this is very easy. You need (1) Certificate of Corporation as issued by the state you're in when you receive your packet in the mail. (2) Corporate resolution authorizing the establishment of a bank account or you can use your (EIN) Employer Identification Number to open up an account. (3) Your initial deposit ($500 to $1,000). This is the amount I advise, but it's no assigned amount you must have to open up an account. The more in your business account, the better and greater your credit lines will be. $500 will get you $5,000 credit line, $1,000 may get you a $10,000 credit line. The more you put in the bigger and greater your business credit lines will be. When I first opened up my business account I placed $5,000 in my business account and received a pre-approved credit line for 50,000. Now that you have read all the information you'll need to build true success, now it's up to you to get up off your behind and start making moves, today. Always remember to put your affairs to the side and take a big step towards becoming your own BOSS and entrepreneur.

Conclusion

We want to thank all our Readers for taking the time out to read this book, "Think Rich". If you have any comments or any suggestions, please feel free to contact us on Facebook on our Authors page. Send us a request and we will get back with you as soon as we can to answer any questions you may have. If you want to pursue your dream and need some advice, read our special tips on our website www.Coyprintpub.com. Think Rich.

It's all about what you know, and who you know. So start connecting now!

By: Kalvin Duker
and
Shacoy McNish

About The Authors

Shacoy McNish is the Founder and C.E.O. of Coy Print Publishing, a Business Consultant who went to school in the State of Pennsylvania, City of Philadelphia for B.O.A. (Business Of Administration). Shacoy McNish mastered the business craft and invested a lot of his time studying many topics, such as, Real Estate, Accounting, Marketing, and much more. His mission is to help others by teaching them how to become C.E.O's. and Entrepreneurs. He set under many corporate lawyers in the business world, and had dealings with thousands of business owners in Philadelphia, New Jersey, Delaware Las Vegas, Florida, and also in Countries outside the United States. To reiterate our mission, it is for us to help people Think Rich, and introduce them to a new way of life.

About The Authors

Born in Cecil County, MD, but raised in the State of Delaware. Kalvin Levon Duker was young ambitious, dedicated and determined to become successful. Growing up with five brothers and one sister. He has always had a strong desire to keep his family structure close knitted an extremely stable with plans to one day have financial freedom. With the knowledge he has acquired in the areas of marketing, Promotion, Business Management, Financial Advising, and Real Estate Investing along with obtaining a Bachelor's Degree in Behavioral Science. Kalvin has always thought and informed his loved one's and close friends to "Think Rich".

You're The Publisher, We're Your Legs

We Offer Editing For An Extra Fee, and Highly Suggest It, If Waved, We Print What You Submit!

Crystell Publications can help you self-publish your novel. Regardless of your status, our team will help you get to print. Our BLOW OUT prices are for serious authors only. **Don't have all your money? No Problem!** *Ask About our Payment Plans*

Crystal Perkins-Stell, MHR
Essence Magazine Bestseller
We Give You Books!
PO BOX 8044 / Edmond – OK 73083
www.crystalstell.com
(405) 414-3991

Hey! Stop Wishing and get your book to print NOW!!!

$674.00 Spring POD Special 250 page Manuscript. Add **$75.00** for custom covers.2 Proofs –Publisher & Printer Copy, Mink Magazine Subscription, Free Advertisement, Book Cover, ISBN #, Conversion, Typeset, Correspondence, Masters, 8 hrs Consultation. ***Inquire about our 100 book plan rates**

Grind Plans 25 & E-Book	Hustle Hard	Respect The Code	313 Deal
Order Extra Books	**$899.00**	**$869.00**	**$839.00**
	255-275pg	250 -205	200 -80
Insanity Plans E-Book & POD	Psycho	Spastic	Mental
Extra Books Can Be Ordered	**$759.00**	**$659.00**	**$559.00**
	225-250pg	200-220	70pgs or less

All Manuscript Options except the E-Books include:
2 Proofs–Printer, Mink Magazine Subscription, Free Advertisement, Book Cover, ISBN #, Conversion, Typeset, Correspondence, Masters, 8 hrs Consultation

$100.00 E-book upload only	**$75** Can't afford edits, Spell-check
$275.00-Book covers/Authors input	**$499** Flat Rate Edits Exceeds 210 add 1.50
$200.00-Book covers/ templates	**$200**-Typeset Book Format PDF File
$190.00 and up Websites	**$200 and up /** Type Manuscript Call for details
$175.00 and up, book trailers	**$1.60** Per Page to Type

We're Changing The Game.

No more paying Vanity Presses $8 to $10 per book! We Give You Books @ Cost.